The Trustee's Guide
TO FIDUCIARY RESPONSIBILITIES

THIRD EDITION, REVISED AND EXPANDED

NAIS Trustee Series

David E. Ormstedt and Debra P. Wilson

David E. Ormstedt was formerly with Wiggin and Dana LLP.
Debra P. Wilson is general counsel at NAIS.

National Association
of Independent Schools

© 2006, 2012, 2016 by the National Association of Independent Schools

This *Trustee's Guide to Fiduciary Responsibilities* is a revised and expanded version of a previous NAIS book, *Holding the Trust: An Independent School Trustee's Guide to Fiduciary Responsibilities*.

ISBN: 978-1-63115-012-8

Printed in the United States of America

The National Association of Independent Schools provides services to more than 1,800 schools and associations of schools in the United States and abroad, including 1,500 nonprofit, private K–12 schools in the U.S. that are self-determining in mission and program and are governed by independent boards. NAIS works to empower independent schools and the students they serve.

For more information, visit the NAIS website at http://www.nais.org.

Editors: Susan Hunt, Karla Taylor
Design: Fletcher Design, Inc./Washington, DC

All rights reserved. No part of this publication may be reproduced, stored in or introduced into a retrieval system, or transmitted in any form or by any means (electronic, mechanical, photocopying, recording, or otherwise) without prior written permission of NAIS. The scanning, uploading, and distribution of this book via the Internet or via any other means without the permission of the publisher is illegal and punishable by law. Brief quotations or excerpts of this publication for use in reviews or professional works are permitted as provided under intellectual property law.

Contents

Introduction 1

PART 1: Existing Legal Framework 7

    STANDARDS OF CONDUCT AND DUTIES OF TRUSTEES, 7
        Duty of care, 8
        Duty of loyalty, 13
        Duty of obedience, 17

    STATE LAWS AFFECTING NONPROFITS, 18
        Uniform Prudent Management of Institutional Funds Act, 18
        Statutes requiring adherence to donor intent, 20

    FEDERAL LAW, 22
        The Internal Revenue Service, 22
        Sarbanes-Oxley, 25

PART 2: Best Governance Practices Not Mandated by Law 27

    THE AUDIT COMMITTEE, 28

    A COMMITTEE TO REVIEW GOVERNANCE ISSUES, 30

    TERM LIMITS FOR TRUSTEES, 30

    PERIODIC REVIEW OF INVESTMENT POLICY AND PERFORMANCE, 31

    MANAGING CONFLICTS OF INTEREST, 31
        Disclosure, 32
        Awareness, 32
        Compliance, 33
        Parent trustees, 33
        Prophylactic effect of compliance with policies, 34

    CONCLUSION, 34

PART 3: Resources, Samples, and Checklists... 37

    NAIS Principles of Good Practice for Boards of Trustees, 38

    NAIS Principles of Good Practice for Independent School Trustees, 40

    Sample Code of Ethics, Code of Conduct, and Conflict of Interest Policy for Trustees, Officers, and Senior Management, 42

    Sample Conflict of Interest Disclosure Statement, 53

    Sample Whistleblower Protection Policy, 56

    Sample Endowment Policy, 58

    Sample Record Retention and Disposal Policy, 61

    Board and Administrative Policy Checklists, 67

    Risk Management Checklist, 69

Introduction

SETTING THE SCENE

The scandals that rocked publicly traded companies in the early 2000s altered operating practices for for-profits and nonprofits alike. WorldCom, Enron, and Tyco became household names. The common elements of their stories included pilfering corporate assets for personal use, deceiving shareholders by cooking the books, and issuing false and misleading financial statements. The schemes to defraud investors went on for so long because few, if any, mechanisms were available for outsiders to detect what was going on. An opaque shield hid the conflicts of interest and the manipulation of financial data. This shield was made possible by corporate cultures in which management's objective was to enrich itself with no regard for its employees, investors, customers, or suppliers.

That culture was aided and abetted by the companies' boards of directors abdicating their responsibilities. In some cases, board members were simply asleep at the switch — failing to pay attention to what was going on in the very corporation they were charged with governing. In other cases, the directors approved excessive executive compensation packages and/or failed to put sufficient checks and balances in place to correct conflicts of interest and financial shenanigans that should have been obvious to even the most casual observer.

The scandals shook the very foundation of investor and public confidence in publicly traded companies. Increasingly and alarmingly, the public couldn't expect management to tell the truth about corporate performance and expectations. Citizens were appalled at the greed exhibited by CEOs, CFOs, COOs, and other company executives in the form of obscenely high compensation and other perquisites. Most troubling was the fact that even if the culture of greed and deception existed in only a small percentage of companies, the distrust threatened to extend across the commercial sector.

And there is a human face to these events: Thousands upon thousands of ordinary people lost their life savings, their retirement, and more because they had mistakenly trusted that the system would protect them.

In response, Congress passed the American Competitiveness and Corporate Accountability Act of 2002, more commonly known as the Sarbanes-Oxley Act (or simply "Sarbanes"). Sarbanes applies to publicly held companies — that is, companies that issue stock that is traded on the various stock exchanges. With two exceptions (protection for whistleblowers and prohibition on document destruction, both discussed later in this book), Sarbanes does not apply to nonprofits. But its tenets have become expected practice for organizations of all types.

Sarbanes focuses on establishing mechanisms to detect fraud during the auditing process and, specifically, to hinder the manipulation of financial data to deceive auditors. Among Sarbanes' requirements:

- Accounting firms engaged in auditing a publicly traded corporation are prohibited from also offering certain other services to the company, such as bookkeeping, technology, and management services.
- Companies must rotate lead and reviewing auditors every five years.
- Companies must create space between the board of directors' Audit Committee and management by requiring that no member of the committee can be an employee of, or otherwise have financial ties to, the company.
- Companies must require that the Audit Committee — not management — hire, compensate, and oversee the auditor.

- The CEO and CFO must certify that the audited financial statements "fairly represent, in all material respects, the operations and financial condition of the issuer."
- The company's annual report must contain a statement from management that no known significant deficiencies in the company's internal financial controls were detected that have not been addressed and resolved.
- At least one member of the Audit Committee must be a financial expert.

SPOTLIGHT ON NONPROFITS

Unfortunately, scandals and the perception of financial abuses resulting from lax governance have not been confined to the commercial sector. As a result, a spotlight is now shining on nonprofits, and a consensus has developed within the sector that trustees and managers of nonprofit organizations need to examine their governance structure and make sure that it supports compliance with current legal obligations and also reflects "best practices." This is in part the result of outside pressure and in part a bona fide desire to do what is necessary and reasonable to insulate the nonprofit sector from the kinds of problems that could lead to the public's loss of confidence in charitable organizations and philanthropy. So while the Sarbanes requirements delineated above are applicable by law only to publicly traded companies, it is now clear that nonprofit corporations, including educational institutions, should be and are incorporating elements of Sarbanes into their governance structure and culture. Indeed, the nonprofit information tax form, the Form 990, received its biggest update in several decades to include management and governance questions that directly address many of these best practices.

Beyond Sarbanes and the ongoing pressure on transparency and disclosure, the nonprofit world was rocked by another type of scandal. In November 2011, Pennsylvania State University found itself under fire for failing to act on an employee report of suspected abuse. The employee reported that he'd seen Jerry Sandusky, one of the school's star football coaches, assaulting a child in a university shower. This initial accusation avalanched into stories of other predatory behavior by Sandusky. On July 12, 2012, an independent investigation report was released, summarily outlining faults in Penn State's processes and policies that allowed such malfeasance to continue unchecked. Among the many issues the investigators identified was a general failure by the board to oversee the risk management and reporting operations of the university in a way that ensured that issues of this nature were brought before the board with full transparency. The report noted that, even with the opportunity to delve more deeply, the board refrained from asking probing questions to learn more about the nature of the accusations and the background behind them.

Indeed, this issue gets to the heart of the tension within nonprofit governance, a board's imperative to lead without undermining management but also to exercise its fiduciary obligations to oversee management's performance and ensure appropriate disclosures. Governance expert Richard Chait, a professor at the Harvard Graduate School of Education, was quoted regarding the Penn State report: "Every board has to strike a balance between two undesirable extremes: one is undue deference and the other is undue interference. That spectrum changes as a result of the issues."[1]

Public opinion is clear: schools have a responsibility for the safety of their constituents. The board has a fiduciary responsibility to ensure that the policies and practices in place support that safety assurance. All schools must track their state laws in this area as the Penn State scandal has caused many states to revisit their reporting requirements, many charging boards and school leaders with greater legal responsibility.

NAIS has produced this manual to help independent school trustees understand their fiduciary responsibilities. The book is divided

---

[1] Quoted in Kevin Kiley, "The Trust of Trustees," *Inside Higher Ed*, July 13, 2012.

into three parts. Part 1 examines the existing legal framework with respect to nonprofit governance and suggests steps nonprofits can take to satisfy not only the letter but also the spirit of the law. Part 2 discusses the governance practices of organizations that recognize that simple compliance with the law is not sufficient to maintain strong constituent confidence in the organization and in philanthropy generally. Part 3 contains sample documents and checklists, which you can adapt as needed for your own school.

This manual should not be construed as legal advice with respect to any particular matter. Rather, it offers general information about the law and best practices in observing the law. Always consult an attorney experienced in nonprofit law for advice on important matters.

Please also note that, for the purposes of this manual, the terms "trustee" and "board of trustees" are interchangeable with the terms "director" and "board of directors," respectively. States occasionally differentiate between the two for legal purposes.

PART 1
Existing Legal Framework

STANDARDS OF CONDUCT AND DUTIES OF TRUSTEES

The trustees of an independent school have duties and responsibilities to the corporation that are grounded in the common law and state statutes. The common law is the set of legal principles derived from decisions rendered by state courts. Statutes are laws that are passed by state legislatures or Congress at the federal level, although, with the exception of the Internal Revenue Code as discussed below, the applicability of federal law to the trustees of nonprofit corporations is limited. State statutes supplement the common law, imposing procedural or substantive requirements not found in the common law. Sometimes, although not often, state statutes replace common law principles.

State statutes and the common law establish the legal framework within which nonprofits operate. For example, statutes will specify how corporations are to be formed in each state, the minimum number of trustees a corporation must have, and the basic required governing documents — most commonly the certificate (or articles) of incorporation and the bylaws.

Together, the certificate of incorporation and the bylaws establish the purpose of the corporation, the number of trustees (usually within a numerical range), the length of their terms, how often the board meets, the number of trustees needed to constitute a quorum for a valid meeting, the number and description of the officers of the board, and the names and duties of the committees of the board. Other items may include whether the corporation has members with certain legal rights (for example, the head of the parents' association may be considered an ex officio member of the board of trustees) and provisions for indemnifying corporate trustees and officers for legal damages incurred while acting on behalf of the corporation. The provisions of these documents supplement and complement state corporate laws that establish the broad parameters under which corporations incorporated in each state may operate.

While the provisions of state statutes and, to some extent, the scope and application of the common law will vary from state to state, there are enough commonalities to generalize the duties of trustees of independent schools throughout the country. These duties are the duty of care, the duty of loyalty, and the duty of obedience.

Duty of Care

A common statement describing the duty of care is that trustees are required (1) to be reasonably informed, (2) to participate in decisions, and (3) to do so in good faith and with the care of an ordinarily prudent person in similar circumstances. To discharge the duty of care, the trustee must be diligent and attentive to the corporation's affairs. This is more than simply monitoring the organization's activities. To properly discharge the duty of care requires active involvement in establishing corporate policies and direction and obtaining information to determine whether those policies and direction are being carried out. This is consistent with the Business Judgment Rule found in state statutes, which provides that a trustee of an independent school shall act (1) in good faith, (2) with the care an ordinarily prudent person in a like position would exercise under similar circumstances, and (3) in a manner the trustee reasonably believes to be in the best interests of the corporation. A trustee is not liable for action taken as a trustee, or for failure to take action, if the trustee complies with the foregoing.

A proper discharge of the duty of care includes the elements described below.

Proper Board Development

The key to success is having the right people at the top governing, guiding, and directing the organization. That means care must be taken in recruiting and evaluating prospective board members. It is not enough that all board members have an interest in the institution, although that would certainly be a prerequisite. It is important that the board be composed of individuals with a proper mix of skills and experience, such as finance and investing. It is also important that prospective members understand what will be expected of them. To that end, it is a good idea to create a written job description for board members, similar to what would be prepared to recruit managers. The job description would include, among other things, the items discussed here involving the discharge of the duty of care.

Finally, it is prudent for the board to provide training to new board members on being a trustee of an independent school, as well as specific background and information about the independent school they are serving. Although prospective nonprofit board members may have served on boards of for-profit corporations, training is still necessary to focus the prospective trustee on the special duties and responsibilities associated with service on a nonprofit board.

A Focus on Purpose and Mission

Every action a board takes must be made with the nonprofit's corporate purpose and mission in mind. In other words, each trustee should decide whether the considered action is consistent with and in furtherance of the purpose of the organization as stated in its governing documents and its mission as articulated by the board. Note that "purpose" and "mission" are not synonymous. An organization's purpose is the goal that the organization is seeking to accomplish, and a statement of purpose explains why the organization exists. A mission, however, is a broader concept, and a mission statement not only includes the purpose but also describes the manner in which the purpose will be achieved and the organization's guiding values.

Stewardship of Resources

Board members have a duty to ensure, to the best of their ability, that the organization has the necessary resources to accomplish its mission, that those resources are rationally allocated, that they are reasonably protected from waste and misappropriation, and that they are invested prudently. In order to fulfill this obligation, board members must understand the school's resources, particularly the financial and human capital, as well as the prioritization of how those resources are used.

Attendance at Meetings

A board should have an attendance policy that encourages members to attend meetings. Trustees cannot adequately exercise their duty of care if they do not regularly attend meetings. This includes meetings of any committee of which they are a member. By way of illustration, the bylaws could provide that a member will be dismissed from the board for missing two consecutive board meetings or any three of eight consecutive meetings. A board that meets three times a year might want to have a more restrictive policy than a board that meets 10 times a year.

For some institutions, an attendance requirement can pose a practical problem. Frequently, the board is composed of individuals who have significant and demanding day jobs whose schedule and work demands interfere with their ability to attend meetings, especially if travel is involved. Adherence to a strict attendance policy may result in such a member being forced off the board. The dilemma for the board is having to choose between losing the services of a talented member, who may also be a substantial contributor with business and social contacts that are beneficial to the school, and maintaining a policy that keeps board members active and engaged.

Put differently, is the value of some board members to the organization related to whether they regularly attend meetings? It may be tempting to answer "no"; however, these individuals, despite their contacts and influence that may help the school, cannot fulfill their fiduciary obligations without participating in meetings of the board. An individual who cannot meet the attendance requirements of the board may be better suited to acting as a special counsel to the board on specific initiatives or endeavors. Alternatively, the board may consider whether using videoconferencing or other technology that allows participants to hear and speak throughout the meeting may help board members fulfill their attendance requirements.

Preparation for Meetings
Members must come prepared for meetings and actively participate in them. Members should be provided with briefing material far enough in advance to give them the opportunity to understand the issues and facts to be addressed at the meeting. But having the opportunity to be prepared is not the same as being prepared. Trustees should read and analyze the material and be ready to ask questions. Trustees may be concerned that they will be perceived as confrontational or lacking in collegiality if they ask tough questions, but if they fail to ask such questions in the face of doubts or inadequate information, they are not exercising the duty of care.

Prudent Delegation of Authority
A trustee's duty of care to the organization is personal. It cannot be transferred to others. A trustee should not, for example, send a business associate to attend a board meeting because the trustee has a schedule conflict, and the board should not permit the delegate to sit. This is not to say, however, that trustees may not rely on professional advice and opinion, such as that of accountants, attorneys, executive compensation analysts, and investment advisors, as long as the trustee has no reason to question the expertise or independence of the person giving the advice. Similarly, a trustee may rely on the advice and conclusions of a committee of the board of which the trustee is not a member — but again, only if the trustee is confident that the committee is knowledgeable about the matter in question, and there is no reason to believe that any member of the committee has a conflict of interest on the matter.

The trustee may also rely on the advice and opinion of an employee or officer of the corporation if the trustee believes that person to be reliable and competent. However, greater care should be exercised with respect to the latter because of the inherent self-interest of management and other compensated employees. This is one of the areas where the Penn State report would suggest that school boards balance the gravity of their responsibility to a vulnerable community with the board's trust and delegation of authority to management. Where issues of child safety and well-being are concerned, boards must remain aware of the risks and strengths of a school's programs and stay well-informed about any issues that arise in this area. Indeed, the ongoing reporting of past abuse cases in independent schools has caused many schools to hire third-party investigators to ensure that investigations and follow-up steps are not tainted by internal conflicts of interest.

Oversight of the Head of School

An important element of the duty of care is hiring, overseeing, and, when circumstances warrant, firing the head of school. Nonprofit boards generally give great deference to the CEO, which, in most cases, is deserved. However, it is always the duty of the board and individual trustees to determine whether the head of school is carrying out the purpose and mission of the organization and the policies and direction set by the board and otherwise acting in the best interests of the institution.

Oversight includes setting reasonable compensation and benefits for the head of school. In the late 1990s, a compensation scandal occurred at Adelphi University in New York State. In 1997, the state education department's board of regents removed 18 of the 19 Adelphi trustees, contending that they had grossly overpaid the school's president, whose annual pay and benefits were reported to exceed $800,000 even though student enrollment was declining. The school's president was ousted, and both the school's new trustees and the New York attorney general sued the former trustees for wasting Adelphi's assets by neglecting their responsibilities, failing to properly oversee and monitor the president's salary, failing to review the president's job performance, and misspending "to support a lavish lifestyle" for the president. The former trustees and the former president agreed to a multimillion-dollar settlement to reimburse the school.

Other examples of similar situations within the nonprofit and education community have been in the news since that time, focusing attention on the need for trustees to take prudent care to ensure that a school's resources are preserved by compensating employees appropriately and reasonably. In the wake of the Adelphi scandal, the IRS passed intermediate sanctions regulations to ensure that nonprofit institutions do just that.

Maintaining Confidentiality
Because of the sensitivity of the information trustees have access to, confidentiality is vitally important. That means trustees must not convey any information to other members of the community, spouses, or friends. Such discretion is imperative for protecting board deliberations and decisions, competitive information about the school, and information related to employees or community members.

Duty of Loyalty

It is a cardinal rule that a trustee must always act in the best interests of the school, without regard to the trustee's personal interest (usually financial) or the personal interest of any other individual. The trustee must not take an opportunity available to the institution and personally exploit it. This does not mean, however, that a person is disqualified to be a trustee simply because there is a reasonable possibility, or even a probability, that at some point a matter of the trustee's personal interest will be affected by an act taken or not taken by the school. Rather, it means that if such a situation arises, the trustee should take all reasonable measures to manage the conflict in the best interest of the institution. The section below provides further discussion of this issue.

Conflicts of Interest
The failure of a board of trustees to be attentive to the possibility of

conflicts of interest between a trustee and a nonprofit combined with the failure to develop mechanisms to deal with conflicts when they arise is a volatile mixture indeed. The scandals in the corporate world mentioned earlier probably would not have happened if the boards of those companies had paid attention to the conflicts issue.

Similarly for nonprofits, the failure to recognize that conflicts of interest may arise in the routine course of the nonprofit's activity or, worse, that a trustee may intentionally seek to push a transaction that will provide financial gain to the trustee, the trustee's business interests, his or her family, or someone else, could very well cause significant damage to the nonprofit. Independent schools rely on the trust of alumni for financial and other support. If it becomes known that a trustee has breached a fiduciary duty by using the school's funds for personal gain, and that the board as a whole failed to take notice because it had not established processes to reasonably identify and avoid the conflict of interest, support for and confidence in the school will likely be severely shaken. Moreover, the incident may draw the attention of the Internal Revenue Service, the state attorney general, or other officials.

That is indeed what happened to The Nature Conservancy, the country's largest "green" organization. Following a series of critical articles in the *Washington Post* in 2003, the U.S. Senate Finance Committee investigated a broad array of Conservancy practices. One alleged practice involved land transactions between the Conservancy and its trustees. The practice was described by the *Washington Post* in a story covering a Senate Finance Committee report on its findings:

> Under the program, the Conservancy purchases land, attaches conservation easement restrictions, and then resells the property at a lesser amount designed to reflect the decrease in land value caused by the restrictions on development. The buyers, in turn, make charitable contributions to cover the difference between the Conservancy's original purchase price and the lower resale price. That cash gift allows the buyers to claim substantial tax breaks.

Such transactions, the report said, "test the limits" of the law, because in most of the deals examined by the Finance Committee it appeared as though the Conservancy would not have sold the property if the buyer had not simultaneously made the cash contribution. The panel questioned whether the buyers could legitimately claim the cash payments as tax-deductible charitable donations....

Until recently, the Conservancy generally did not market the properties to the public, but instead sold many of the tracts to its trustees, staff members and other supporters, the report said. The report questioned whether the buyers, who often helped craft the terms of the land deals, paid less than full price for the tracts.[2]

In response to the criticism, The Nature Conservancy convened an expert advisory committee to recommend ways it could strengthen its governance, transparency, and accountability. Among the measures adopted by the Conservancy is a revised conflict of interest policy that prohibits land transactions with its trustees and other related parties. When the IRS revisited the Form 990 filed by all nonprofits above a certain financial threshold, the revised form included questions about whether the nonprofit has a conflict of interest policy.

Sources of Conflicts of Interest

The following briefly discusses the most likely sources of conflicting interests. Suggestions on how to manage those conflicts will be offered later.

Personal financial interest. A frequent source of conflicting interests is when a trustee or a relative of a trustee has an ownership in, or an employment relationship with, an entity proposing to do business with the independent school. Common examples are insurance policies, banking and investment services, and accounting work. Another

---

[2] Joe Stephens and David Ottaway, "Senators Question Conservancy's Practices," *Washington Post*, June 8, 2005.

example of personal financial conflict is when a head of school or other top management official uses a person's influence to extract excessive compensation or benefits from the nonprofit. Nonmanagerial employees of the nonprofit may also have financial interests in a company with which the nonprofit is considering a transaction. The financial interest may be an ownership share of the company or the receipt of gifts of merchandise or entertainment from the company.

A landmark example of the first situation is a case involving Sibley Memorial Hospital. In a class action lawsuit, patients of the hospital successfully sued the hospital's trustees. The trustees were charged with, among other things, breach of duty by mismanaging assets and by self-dealing, or taking advantage of their position and acting in their own interests instead of the hospital's. It was alleged that a substantial amount of the hospital's money was in savings and checking accounts earning little or no interest at banks with which some of the hospital trustees were affiliated. To make matters worse, those trustees had failed to disclose their relationships with the banks to the full board.

On a less dramatic level, many independent school trustees find themselves with the inherent conflict of being a parent of a student in the school. These individuals are often faced with voting on raising tuition costs and other such steps that may affect them financially. Generally, most independent school boards do not consider this a substantial conflict of interest but do balance out current parents on the board with others from the community who do not have such inherent tension.

Nonfinancial interest. It is not unusual for a trustee of an independent school to also serve as a trustee of one or more other nonprofits. Situations could arise where one corporation's action or inaction could either benefit or damage the interests of another nonprofit of which the trustee is a board member. A trustee may also be employed by another nonprofit whose interests could be favorably or adversely affected by an act of the trustee's board. This situation arises when an employee from one school sits on the board of another school.

Parent trustees also face unusual nonfinancial conflicts of interest.

The most common of these involves a parent trustee's personal conflict over management steps the head of school may take when faced with internal management decisions, particularly those relating to personnel. Beyond personnel issues, these trustees often find themselves conflicted over issues involving other parents or students, particularly when disciplinary decisions made by the school are in question. The IRS now asks all nonprofits to report on Form 990 whether they have a conflict of interest policy and how the policy works.

Duty of Obedience

The duty of obedience requires that a trustee be faithful to the purpose and mission of the organization the trustee serves. As noted, the purpose of the nonprofit is set forth in its governing documents, such as the certificate (or articles) of incorporation and the bylaws. The mission is articulated by the board in the organization's mission statement. The purpose and mission of the organization are expressed elsewhere as well. In its application to the Internal Revenue Service for tax-exempt status, a nonprofit is required to describe its purpose and its planned program activities. Another expression of the organization's purpose and mission is found in its appeals for contributions, wherein donors are told why funds are needed and how they will be used. Trustees should take great care to ensure that the nonprofit's assets are used in a manner that is consistent with the governing documents and the representations made to its constituents and the general public.

A Connecticut case illustrates this principle. The trustees of a museum in southeastern Connecticut devised a plan to relocate the museum and its assets to Rhode Island. The museum had been created and sustained in substantial part by contributions from the southeastern Connecticut community. The state attorney general sued to block the move, charging, among other things, that the museum's certificate of incorporation specified that the corporation's geographic service area was southeastern Connecticut and so the move to Rhode Island would violate the corporation's purpose. The case was settled when the attorney general agreed to permit the trustees to move a small portion of the museum's assets to a new facility in Rhode Island, in exchange for which the museum trustees agreed to transfer all the rest of the museum's assets to a new corporation with a new board of trustees that would continue to operate the existing Connecticut facility.

Many schools stumble across similar issues when the original purpose of a gift, either money or grounds, is no longer appropriate for the future practices of the school (e.g., a school raises money for the education of boys, but time passes and eventually the school becomes coeducational).

The duty of obedience further requires that trustees see to it that the nonprofit is operated in compliance with all laws to which it is subject. While there are many such laws, common examples affecting nonprofits are employment laws, tax laws concerning employee withholding and the annual filing of IRS Form 990, and occupational health and safety laws. While it is certainly neither possible nor expected that trustees can ensure that management is complying with all laws in all respects, the board should establish procedures by which trustees can monitor whether management is being attentive to its legal obligations.

STATE LAWS AFFECTING NONPROFITS

All states have statutes that address specific aspects of the operation of nonprofits. Two of the most common are described below.

Uniform Prudent Management of Institutional Funds Act (UPMIFA)

Starting in 1972, the Uniform Management of Institutional Funds Act (UMIFA) applied to funds held by charitable organizations, including endowment. It was adopted in some form by all states except Alaska, Pennsylvania, and South Dakota. The act provided guidance on investment authority, permitted delegation of authority to independent financial advisors, authorized the expenditure of appreciation on investment funds, and provided rules for the release of restrictions on the use or investment of funds. This law was updated in 2006 in the Uniform Prudent Management of Institutional Funds Act, which has been adopted by all states except Pennsylvania.

Under UPMIFA, the members of a governing board must still exercise ordinary business care and prudence under the facts and circumstances prevailing at the time of the investment action or decision. In making an investment decision, the board must consider, among other things, (1) the long- and short-term needs of the organization in carrying out its charitable purpose, (2) the organization's present and anticipated financial requirements, (3) the expected total return on its investments, (4) price-level trends, and (5) general economic conditions.

While it is outside the scope of this publication to analyze UMIFA and UPMIFA, two elements deserve attention. The first involves the prudent investing and use of the fund. UMIFA authorized the governing board of a charitable organization to appropriate for expenditure, for the uses and purposes for which an endowment fund is established, so much of the net appreciation, realized and unrealized, in the value of the assets of an endowment fund over the historic dollar value of the fund as is prudent. The historic dollar value of the fund is the original amount of the gift plus any additional contributions made to it over the years. Unlike UMIFA, UPMIFA allows a board to authorize expenditures from the fund that would cause its value to fall below its historic dollar value.

In general, to be prudent, a board should consider at least the following 10 factors in deciding whether to spend or accumulate appreciation:

1. Duration and preservation of the fund
2. Purposes of the institution and of the fund
3. General economic conditions
4. Possible effect of inflation or deflation
5. Expected total return from income and appreciation
6. Other resources of the institution that are available for use

7. The investment policy of the institution
8. Expected tax consequences
9. The needs of the institution and the fund to make distributions or preserve capital
10. The asset's special relationship or value to the charitable purposes of the institution

These 10 factors are expanded from UMIFA's original approach and allow for a more modern approach to portfolio management where all of the assets are considered as part of the whole. Most institutions take the factors into consideration by adopting and adhering to a reasonable spending rule.

The second important change between UMIFA and UPMIFA relates to the duty to oversee the management of the fund. UPMIFA provides that a person with special skills or expertise, such as a trustee or investment advisor hired by the institution, has a duty to utilize such skills in managing the fund, be it in actively managing the fund or overseeing an advisor. UPMIFA also provides for a duty to manage costs. Under UPMIFA, an institution may incur costs only if they are reasonable in light of the institution's assets, purposes, and available skills. In addition, the duty to investigate requires an institution to make a reasonable effort to verify the facts being relied upon in making investment decisions. This includes exercising prudence in choosing an advisor or investment agent, delineating the scope of such agency, and reviewing such agent's activities from time to time for compliance. The reasonableness of the costs associated with managing the funds has become an important question for nonprofits, particularly relative to the same obligation found in the oversight of retirement plans of nonprofits.

Statutes Requiring Adherence to Donor Intent

It is a settled principle, grounded in common law dating from the 1601 English Statute of Elizabeth, that a gift must be used in accordance with the intent of the donor. The purpose of this principle is to promote and encourage philanthropy by instilling confidence in donors that their gifts will be used as they intended. The principle applies to all gifts, whether fully expendable on a current basis or an endowment fund.

Every nonprofit that has received gifts restricted by its grantors, including restrictions regarding when and for what purpose the principal or income may be spent, should have a process to document the gifts and their restrictions, as well as to be able to track income to, and expenditures from, the funds. This is not only necessary from a legal viewpoint; it is also necessary for the auditor to be able to issue a "clean" opinion on the organization's financial statements. A good practice is for the board to acknowledge receipt of gifts, and the restrictions placed by the donors on their use, in its meeting minutes.

Note that this principle applies only to gifts whose use has been restricted by the donor. It does not apply to funds that have been designated by the board of trustees as endowment (variously called board-designated endowment, funds acting as endowment, or quasi-endowment).

It is not uncommon for nonprofits to use restricted funds for general operating expenses in times of financial hardship or to initiate a new program without adequate unrestricted funds to pay for it. But the law does not permit this practice. Organizations also sometimes "borrow" from restricted funds, and while this practice is not generally illegal per se, there are substantial risks and it's generally frowned upon. If the restricted income is borrowed, then it's not available to be spent for the purpose designated by the donor of the fund. If all or a portion of accumulated appreciation is borrowed, then the fund will produce proportionately less investment income for use as the donor intended. It is also never a good idea to borrow from a fund so as to cause its value to fall below its historic dollar value.

At a minimum, the decision about whether to borrow should be made by the board and documented in its minutes, and a timetable for repayment of the loan with market-rate interest should be established. Keep in mind, however, that the board will need to be certain that it will be able to come up with new unrestricted money from other sources to replenish the fund.

It is also not uncommon for an organization to find that it's no longer possible, or practical, to use a gift for the purpose imposed by the donor. Although the process varies by state, as a general rule, a state court can release or modify the restriction on the basis of evidence that, due to changed circumstances, it is no longer legal, possible, or practicable to use the gift as the donor intended. Under a legal doctrine known as *cy pres* ("as close as possible"), the court will approve another use of the fund that satisfies the general charitable intent of the donor. Under UPMIFA, a fund's restriction on management of investment, or on its use or charitable purpose, may be released or modified by a court or by the donor's written consent. Additionally, if a fund meets the definition of being "old" and "small," the organization may alter the fund, consistent with the charitable purposes of the instrument, simply by providing notice to the state attorney general. UPMIFA allows this type of release for funds under $25,000 in value and more than 20 years old, the theory being that sufficient time has passed that notification of the donor would be impracticable and court approval would be disproportionately costly. (In adopting UPMIFA, some states have defined "small" as less than $50,000 or even $100,000.)

FEDERAL LAW

The Internal Revenue Service

The IRS affects independent schools in two ways: the Form 990 and intermediate sanctions.

The Form 990: The Annual Information Return

Charitable organizations, including schools, that the IRS has determined to be exempt from income taxation under section 501(c)(3) of the Internal Revenue Code — and to which tax-deductible donations may be made — must file an annual information return with the IRS on Form 990. The form includes the organization's revenue and expenses, a breakdown of expenses by category, a balance sheet, a statement of program service accomplishments, and other information. The Form 990 requires charities to disclose the total compensation (salary and value of benefits) paid to highly compensated employees.

As already mentioned, the updated 990 now requires disclosures that were not required before 2008. The new form asks governance and management questions, such as whether the nonprofit has a document destruction policy, a whistleblower policy, and a conflict of interest policy, as well as whether the nonprofit engages in steps designed to ensure that the compensation paid to employees is reasonable.

The Form 990 is a public document. With certain exceptions, a charity is required to provide copies of its three most recent returns to anyone upon request. Also, several years of returns can be reviewed and downloaded from the website *www.guidestar.org*.

Intermediate Sanctions

Prior to 1995, the only way the IRS could punish a charity whose assets were diverted to private gain was to revoke the tax-exempt status of the organization. To give the IRS greater enforcement flexibility, Congress enacted what is commonly referred to as "intermediate sanctions" legislation. This legislation permits the IRS to levy an excise tax on individuals who receive excessively rich economic benefits from a charity and on individuals who knowingly approve the excess benefit, which could include board members. The tax is not on the charity itself.

The sanctions apply to transactions in which an insider received a financial benefit that exceeds the value the charity received from the transaction. The excise tax is applied to the "excess benefit" received by the insider — or the value that exceeds the fair market value of the money, goods, or services. For example, if a school has paid $50,000 for insurance policies purchased annually from an agency owned by John, who is on the school's board of trustees, but John's agency normally charges $30,000 to other clients for the same coverage, a tax will be levied on John. The initial tax is 25 percent of the $20,000 difference, or $5,000, and the excess benefit must be returned to the school. If

John does not reimburse the difference to the charity within a certain period of time, an additional 200 percent tax is levied on him, for a total of $45,000. In addition, a 10 percent tax on the difference or $10,000, whichever is less, is levied on any "organization manager" who participated in approving the transactions and who knew the amounts paid were excessive. If, say, a committee of the board unanimously approved the transactions, each member of the committee is subject to the 10 percent tax, or $2,000 in this case.

The intermediate sanctions tax also applies to compensation packages of insiders, or "disqualified persons" as the law calls them. These persons are generally the officers and trustees of the organization and other persons in a position to exercise substantial influence over the affairs of the nonprofit. In a school, the head of the school is always a disqualified person. In most schools, the business officer will also be a disqualified person. Other individuals may also fall into this category, depending on their duties. Thus, if the board approves an excessive compensation package for the head, the head and each board member who did not affirmatively oppose the package are liable for the tax.

To protect itself, a board can create a "rebuttable presumption" that a compensation package is reasonable. The IRS has issued guidance on how that can be done. The following is excerpted from that guidance:

> The board of trustees, or other compensation-setting body, must obtain compensation comparability data for the position. If an organization uses a compensation-setting body, it must be composed of members of the board of trustees unless state law authorizes other persons to perform that function. The members who participate may not have any personal interest in the compensation arrangement. For example, neither the employee whose compensation is at issue, nor the employee's subordinate, may participate in the decision about the compensation. Because each member of the compensation-setting body must be disinterested, the body may be differently constituted depending on the employee whose compensation is under review.
>
> The comparability data may be based on industry surveys, documented compensation of persons holding similar positions

in similar organizations, expert compensation studies, or other comparable data. The decision-making body must approve the compensation, without discussion or voting participation by the person whose compensation is being approved or any other member with a conflict of interest. However, that person may answer questions that will help the decision-making body in its later deliberations.

The decision-making body must document the basis for its determination concurrently with the approval. The documentation must contain:

1. the terms of the approved transaction and the date approved;
2. the members of the decision-making body who were present during debate on the approved transaction and those who voted on it;
3. the comparability data that was relied on by the decision-making body and how the data was obtained; and
4. any actions by a member of the decision-making body having a conflict of interest.

The documentation must be prepared before the next meeting of the decision-making body, or 60 days after the final action of the body, whichever is later. In addition, the decision-making body must approve the documentation within a reasonable time after preparation.[3]

The intermediate sanctions regulations are intricate and complex. The foregoing is not intended to be, and should not be construed as, a complete description of their terms. As always, a nonprofit should seek expert legal advice.

Sarbanes-Oxley

As noted earlier, nonprofit organizations are subject to two provisions of Sarbanes-Oxley ("Sarbanes"):

---

[3] Internal Revenue Service, "Rebuttable Presumption – Intermediate Sanctions," March 14, 2016; online at https://www.irs.gov/charities-non-profits/charitable-organizations/rebuttable-presumption-intermediate-sanctions.

Whistleblower Protection

Sarbanes prohibits a corporation from retaliating against an individual who reports suspected illegal activity. To help ensure compliance, each nonprofit should adopt a written policy on handling employee and volunteer complaints, which should be included in the employee manual. People who want to make a complaint should know how to do so, and they should feel confident that a system is in place to address their complaint and that they are safe from retaliation. All managers and supervisors should be aware of this Sarbanes requirement.

Document Destruction

Sarbanes makes it a crime to alter, hide, destroy, or falsify documents to prevent their use in litigation or official proceedings. Every nonprofit should develop a document retention and destruction policy and adhere to it. It is helpful to develop the policy in consultation with the organization's auditors. One element of the policy should be that no documents are destroyed once the nonprofit knows, or has reason to know, that a government investigation of the organization has begun.

PART 2
Best Governance Practices Not Mandated by Law

The first part of this manual provided an overview of the legal obligations of independent schools' trustees. But nonprofits are increasingly expected to do more than simply comply with the letter of the law. Indeed, it is in their best interest to seek out and adopt best practices, to the extent those practices are reasonable in light of the organization's nature and purpose. If poor governance structure and oversight create conditions that allow a board's actions to be called into question, it will be of little solace to disaffected constituents that the board complied with the law.

When assessing an organization's governance structure and culture, the board should keep these points in mind:

- Analysis of board structure is not about assessing the passion, sincerity, and dedication of board members. Rather, it is about determining whether the governance structure supports and encourages the qualities that individual board members bring to the table. It is about looking for checks and balances and the prudent allocation of authority.

- A board should resist the temptation to simply measure itself against what may be common practice at similar institutions. A premier institution will seek to align itself with evolving thinking and adopt changes that will make its governance structure and processes sound.

- Publicly traded businesses and nonprofit organizations are not so fundamentally different as to preclude parallels between the two. Both have constituencies upon whom they depend and whose trust and confidence they must cultivate and preserve. Although the Sarbanes-Oxley legislation that emanated from the business controversies does not generally apply to nonprofits, expert commentary and recent developments make it clear that the requirements of that legislation are being drawn upon as nonprofit institutions rethink and transform their governance structures from what has been to what should be. For example, Drexel University adopted broad governance reforms in 2003. The following is an excerpt from the university's announcement:

  > We are not a public corporation, but we do the public's business. ... We have always aspired to conduct the affairs of this University at the highest levels of ethics, integrity and accountability. The actions we have taken today are a formal commitment to ensure that the best practices used by business will be applied by this University.

The following recommendations are modeled on Sarbanes and reflect the trends and best practices in nonprofit governance. Again, many of these suggestions are now reflected in the Form 990 required of most nonprofit organizations. Although the IRS has recognized that these recommendations are not found in law, representatives from the IRS have generally stated that good governance and management generally lead to good nonprofit tax compliance.

THE AUDIT COMMITTEE

All institutions that have their financial statements audited should have an Audit Committee that operates in accordance with the following:

- This committee should select the auditor and establish the auditor's compensation. The committee should receive, discuss, and approve the audited financial statements, the auditor's report thereon, and the IRS Form 990. It should evaluate on an ongoing basis the efficiency of the school's internal financial controls. All members of the committee can be trustees of the school. All members of the committee should be independent, meaning that (1) no member of management, including the head, may sit on the committee, and (2) no one who has received compensation of any kind from the school in the last three years may be a member. At least one member of the Audit Committee should be a financial expert.

- This committee should meet at least twice each year, with adequate time to review all pertinent information prior to each meeting and adequate time to prepare a report to the full board prior to the board meeting at which the audit results will be discussed. A copy of the audit, the management letter from the auditor pointing out any internal control or other deficiencies identified by the auditor, and the IRS Form 990 should all be provided to the full board for review.

- A school may feel that its board does not have a member or members with sufficient financial literacy to form an Audit Committee. In that case and if state law permits, it may form an Audit Committee composed in part of nonvoting, non-staff advisors who are not on the board although at least one trustee should serve on the committee as its chair. Before doing this, the school should consult legal counsel or its state attorney general to determine whether this is permissible.

- The selected auditor generally should not provide non-auditing services to the organization. However, certain services ancillary to the audit, such as preparation of the IRS Form 990, are permissible. The Audit Committee should approve all non-auditing services. Auditing firms should be rotated periodically. At a minimum, the lead audit partner and lead review partner should be rotated off the engagement after five years. Furthermore, the committee should be prohibited from hiring an auditor if any of the organization's senior management was employed by the auditing firm and

participated in any capacity in an audit of the school within one year before the initiation of the audit.
- The head of school and the business officer should certify to the Audit Committee that the financial statements are presented fairly in all material aspects and that there are no known significant control deficiencies or instances of fraud that have not been addressed and resolved.

A COMMITTEE TO REVIEW GOVERNANCE ISSUES

There should be a standing committee responsible for reviewing and evaluating on an ongoing basis the governance structure of the school and its effectiveness in light of best practices as they evolve in the nonprofit field. Such a committee is often called the Governance Committee. It should recommend, as necessary, structural and procedural changes with respect to the board. To maintain the committee's independence, no member of management, including the head, should be a committee member. The Governance Committee, in cooperation with the Audit Committee, should also create and submit for the board's approval an ethics code for board members, management, and employees. The code should be crafted in such a fashion that makes it clear that the board is setting a tone for exemplary ethics throughout the entire organization and all persons who do business with it.

TERM LIMITS FOR TRUSTEES

The argument against term limits for board service is that they result in experienced and valuable trustees with institutional memory being forced off the board. That is certainly true. On the other hand, long-entrenched board members sometimes tend to dominate the board, marginalizing newer members. Also, there is the danger that over time they will develop too close a relationship with the head, thus impairing their objectivity and hence their ability to effectively fulfill their obligation to oversee and evaluate the head. As Boston University found in 2004, implementing term limits removes individuals who have been on the board for decades and thus removes the perception of governance problems or undue influence related to such long-term service.

PERIODIC REVIEW OF INVESTMENT POLICY AND PERFORMANCE

The full board should approve an investment policy for the organization. While the board may, and probably should, delegate investment functions consistent with that policy to management or an outside investment advisor, the board should periodically review investment goals, activities, and results, especially if the board does not have an Investment Committee. If there is an Investment Committee, it can provide primary oversight, but it is essential that a report be made to the full board from time to time to enable all trustees to assess whether the investment policy is being followed and whether results are meeting expectations.

MANAGING CONFLICTS OF INTEREST

Every nonprofit should have a conflict of interest policy to raise awareness of, and help guard against, potential conflicts that could result in legal problems with the IRS and state government officials; public embarrassment; and the disaffection of alumni, donors, and other constituencies. The IRS has published a sample conflict of interest policy, and another sample is appended to this manual. The following provisions are included:

- Disclosure by interested persons of financial interests and all material facts relating thereto. "Interested person" means any trustee, principal officer, or member of a committee with board-delegated powers who has a direct or an indirect financial interest.
- Procedures for determining whether the financial concerns of the interested person may result in a conflict of interest.

- Procedures for addressing the conflict of interest after determining that there is a conflict. Generally, after providing any information the board requests, the trustee with the conflict must leave the room during the board's discussion and its vote on the matter.
- Procedures for adequate record keeping. The minutes of the board meetings and all committee meetings should include the names of the persons who disclosed potentially conflicting interests, the nature of the potentially conflicting interests, whether the board determined that there was a conflict of interest, the names of all persons present for discussions or votes relating to the transaction or arrangement, the content of these discussions, and a record of the vote.
- Procedures ensuring that the policy is distributed to all trustees and individuals with board-delegated powers. Each such person should sign an annual statement that he or she has received a copy of the conflict of interest policy, has read and understands the policy, agrees to comply with the policy, and understands that the policy applies to all committees and subcommittees having board-delegated powers.

Disclosure

Disclosure is a critical element in ensuring that conflicts are identified and properly managed. Generally, disclosure should occur in two situations: annually in a written disclosure (i.e., a questionnaire) and whenever a conflict of interest arises (before the board takes action). At times, a trustee's fiduciary duty to another person or organization may prevent the trustee from disclosing the nature of the conflict. In such cases, the trustee should at least state that such an interest exists and abstain from participating in the discussion and vote.

Awareness

Trustees must be sensitive to any interest they may have in a decision made by the board and, if possible, recognize the interest prior to the discussion or presentation of the matter before the board.

Compliance

Conflict of interest questionnaires will be useless if trustees are not required to return them. Without these completed questionnaires, there is no mechanism to ensure that trustees are appropriately disclosing potential conflicts; there is no person or committee ensuring that conflicts are appropriately disclosed when they arise; and there is no one to ensure that conflicts are periodically monitored.

Parent Trustees

Schools may also want to consider some of the following steps when approaching the conflicts of interest presented by parent trustees in particular:

- Openly acknowledge the inherent financial and potential personal conflicts created when parents serve on a school board.
- Work to balance the number of parents and non-parents on the board so that the board has a voice that is truly conflict-free. Beyond helping avoid major governance problems that may result from personal conflicts inherent in parent members, non-parent board members are often very useful to the school because they can be more readily involved in reviewing financial aid awards processes, working with the head in tough employment decisions, and addressing other areas that may be inappropriate for parent involvement. Often, former parents or alumni without students are happy to serve in this capacity.
- Create a procedure by which everyone is reminded that, although a financial conflict may not exist, a personal conflict may exist for the parent trustees. Depending upon the nature and extent of the conflict, individual trustees will need to recuse themselves or be asked by the chair of the Governance Committee to recuse themselves.

Prophylactic Effect of Compliance with Policies

Compliance with conflict of interest policies is essential to ensuring entitlement to available protection from liability.

- State statutes offering trustees protection against liability, including liability to the corporation, generally include some variation of a standard that makes the protection available only if the trustee acted in good faith, with the care that an ordinarily prudent person in a like position would exercise under similar circumstances, and in a manner the trustee reasonably believed to be in the best interest of the corporation. If trustees (or business associates or close family members) receive an improper personal economic gain, or if trustees negligently approve an improper transaction with an insider without having and enforcing an effective conflicts policy, the trustees may not be protected from personal liability.

- Coverage requirements in a typical trustees and officers insurance ("D&O" [directors and officers]) policy require trustees and officers to meet similar standards of conduct and care in order to be entitled to be defended and covered by the insurer.

- Trustees, officers, and top management will receive some protection from the imposition of IRS intermediate sanctions if, in the case of an insider transaction or financial arrangement, the conflict is identified in advance of board approval and certain requirements, including outside independent confirmation of the fairness of the value, are met.

CONCLUSION

Trusteeship is a solemn responsibility. Whether the educational institution has the resources and proper leadership to accomplish its mission is largely in the hands of its trustees. To do the job the right way requires time, effort, diligence, thought, attentiveness, and knowledge of the principles of good nonprofit governance. It is a responsibility that cannot be delegated to others. Trustees are ultimately responsible for the excellence of the institution. While management has its responsibilities, it is the trustees who are charged with the responsibility of providing management with the resources and guidance to do its job correctly.

In short, the job of the board of trustees is to govern, and the job of each individual trustee is to work in concert with the other trustees to make sure that the board governs effectively and does no harm to the institution.

PART 3
Resources, Samples, and Checklists

NAIS Principles of Good Practice for Boards of Trustees

Preamble: The following Principles of Good Practice (PGPs) provide common ground for interaction between independent school professionals and their many constituents (parents, students, colleagues at other schools, and the public). The NAIS Principles of Good Practice for member schools define high standards and ethical behavior in key areas of school operations to guide schools in becoming the best education communities they can be; to embed the expectation of professionalism; and to further our sector's core values of transparency, excellence, and inclusivity. Accordingly, membership in NAIS is contingent upon agreement to abide by "the spirit" of the PGPs.

Overview: The board is the guardian of the school's mission. It is the board's responsibility to ensure that the mission is relevant and vital to the community it serves and to monitor the success of the school in fulfilling its mission.

Principles of Good Practice:

1. The board adopts a clear statement of the school's mission, vision, and strategic goals and establishes policies and plans consistent with this statement.
2. The board reviews and maintains appropriate bylaws that conform to legal requirements, including duties of loyalty, obedience, and care.
3. The board ensures that the school and the board operate in compliance with applicable laws and regulations, minimizing exposure to legal action. The board creates a conflict of interest policy that is reviewed with, and signed by, individual trustees annually.
4. The board accepts accountability for both the financial stability and the financial future of the institution, engaging in strategic financial planning, assuming primary responsibility for the preservation of capital assets and endowments, overseeing operating budgets, and participating actively in fund-raising.

5. The board selects, supports, nurtures, evaluates, and sets appropriate compensation for the head of school.
6. The board recognizes that its primary work and focus are long-range and strategic.
7. The board undertakes formal strategic planning on a periodic basis, sets annual goals related to the plan, and conducts annual written evaluations for the school, the head of school, and the board itself.
8. The board keeps full and accurate records of its meetings, committees, and policies and communicates its decisions widely, while keeping its deliberations confidential.
9. Board composition reflects the strategic expertise, resources, and perspectives (past, present, future) needed to achieve the mission and strategic objectives of the school.
10. The board works to ensure that all its members are actively involved in the work of the board and its committees.
11. As leader of the school community, the board engages proactively with the head of school in cultivating and maintaining good relations with school constituents as well as the broader community and exhibits best practices relevant to equity and justice.
12. The board is committed to a program of professional development that includes annual new trustee orientation, ongoing trustee education and evaluation, and board leadership succession planning.

NAIS Principles of Good Practice for Independent School Trustees

Preamble: The following Principles of Good Practice (PGPs) provide common ground for interaction between independent school professionals and their many constituents (parents, students, colleagues at other schools, and the public). The NAIS Principles of Good Practice for member schools define high standards and ethical behavior in key areas of school operations to guide schools in becoming the best education communities they can be; to embed the expectation of professionalism; and to further our sector's core values of transparency, excellence, and inclusivity. Accordingly, membership in NAIS is contingent upon agreement to abide by "the spirit" of the PGPs.

Overview: The following Principles of Good Practice are set forth to provide a common perspective on the responsibilities of individual members of independent school boards.

Principles of Good Practice:

1. A trustee actively supports and promotes the school's mission, vision, strategic goals, and policy positions.
2. A trustee is knowledgeable about the school's mission and goals, including its commitment to equity and justice, and represents them appropriately and accurately within the community.
3. A trustee stays fully informed about current operations and issues by attending meetings regularly, coming to meetings well prepared, and participating fully in all matters.
4. The board sets policy and focuses on long-range and strategic issues. An individual trustee does not become involved directly in specific management, personnel, or curricular issues.
5. The trustee takes care to separate the interests of the school from the specific needs of a particular child or constituency.
6. A trustee accepts and supports board decisions. Once a decision has been made, the board speaks with one voice.

7. A trustee keeps all board deliberations confidential.
8. A trustee guards against conflict of interest, whether personal or business related.
9. A trustee has the responsibility to support the school and its head and to demonstrate that support within the community.
10. Authority is vested in the board as a whole. A trustee who learns of an issue of importance to the school has the obligation to bring it to the head of school, or to the board chair, and must refrain from responding to the situation individually.
11. A trustee contributes to the development program of the school, including strategic planning for development, financial support, and active involvement in annual and capital giving.
12. Each trustee, not just the treasurer and finance committee, has fiduciary responsibility to the school for sound financial management.

Sample Code of Ethics, Code of Conduct, and Conflict of Interest Policy for Trustees, Officers, and Senior Management

This policy combines a Code of Ethics, Code of Conduct, and Conflict of Interest Policy into one document. Rather than having separate policies for the board and senior staff, this model uses just one policy to cover everyone. It refers to a whistleblower protection policy, which is a separate policy. If you use this sample policy, be sure to replace "ABC School" with the name of your school.

ABC SCHOOL
CODE OF ETHICS, CODE OF CONDUCT, AND CONFLICT OF INTEREST POLICY FOR TRUSTEES, OFFICERS, AND SENIOR MANAGEMENT

I. CODE OF ETHICS

ABC School demands the highest possible ethical conduct from individuals serving as its trustees, officers, and senior personnel ("senior management"). Your full compliance with this code is mandatory. You are expected to foster a culture of transparency, integrity, and honesty and to ensure that everyone who reports to you also fully complies with this code.

Construction and Implementation

The provisions of this code are intended to be broadly construed in accordance with the purpose of this code. The board shall be responsible for implementing these provisions and advising persons as to their application. Any person may file with the head of school or the chair of the board a complaint alleging a violation of this code by submitting a written statement setting forth the facts on which the complaint is based. The person submitting a complaint may request an advisory opinion regarding interpretation of the provisions of this code and its application. The complaint and/or request shall set forth the facts upon which the complaint and/or request is based. The head of school and/or the board shall be responsible for making a determination and/or rendering an opinion in accordance with the procedures contained in this code within thirty (30) days of the request or complaint. If a complaint relates to a board member, such board member may not participate in the process of determining whether he or she has a conflict or appearance of a conflict on any matter subject to this code.

Public Disclosures

Public disclosure of certain information about the school is part of the school's general philosophy. It is the school's policy to make full, fair, accurate, timely, and understandable disclosures in its public statements such as press releases.

Periodic Reports to the Board

In compliance with state law and in keeping with the spirit of full disclosure, it is the school's policy to regularly provide to the board of trustees full, fair, accurate, and timely reports and provide them with access to all corporate records in accordance with these guidelines:

- The school's trustees have an absolute right to inspect and copy all books, records, and documents of every kind and to inspect all physical properties owned or leased by the school.
- Each trustee will receive a copy of the annual audited financial statement no later than 120 days after the close of the fiscal year. The audited financial statement shall include, in appropriate detail, the following:
  - The assets and liabilities, including any trust funds, as of the end of the fiscal year
  - The principal changes in assets and liabilities, including any trust funds, during the fiscal year
  - Revenue, both restricted and unrestricted, for the fiscal year
  - Expenses, for both general and restricted purposes, for the fiscal year
- Each trustee will receive an annual report of any transactions with interested persons worth over $10,000 in the aggregate or any indemnification or advance over $10,000 in the aggregate to any trustee or officer.

II. CODE OF CONDUCT

This code of conduct is intended to be used in concert with the school's governing documents, including its articles of incorporation, bylaws, and such policies as the board may adopt as well as applicable state law. It outlines a set of fundamental principles, whether or not they are the basis for certain operational or legal requirements or prohibitions.

These principles are intended to help senior management understand why the school's documents direct behavior in certain ways, why the laws require or prohibit certain actions, and what is to be done when the governing documents and legal strictures are ambiguous or subject to interpretation.

This code of conduct addresses the values of the school and how they reflect the values of the larger society. It helps senior management define what is right, fair, just, and good in those cases where it may be less than obvious which path constitutes the high road.

Personal Ethics. Senior management is expected to behave morally according to general expectations of any person in any society, acting in any capacity. The principles of personal ethics are listed below:

- Concern for the well-being of others
- Respect for the autonomy of others
- Trustworthiness and honesty
- Compliance with the law
- Basic justice: being fair
- Refusal to take unfair advantage
- Benevolence: doing good
- Prevention of harm

Professional Ethics. An individual acting as a senior management member takes on an additional burden of ethical responsibility. Senior management members follow rules of conduct and standards of behavior based on the principles of professional ethics:

- Impartiality
- Openness and full disclosure

- Confidentiality
- Due diligence and duty of care
- Fidelity to professional responsibilities
- Avoidance of potential or apparent conflict of interest

III. CONFLICT OF INTEREST POLICY

All senior management members must avoid any personal activity, investment, or association that could appear to interfere with good judgment concerning the school's best interests and must not exploit their positions or relationships with the school for personal gain. In this regard, the school acknowledges the importance of having a comprehensive policy for identifying and effectively handling potential "conflicts of interest" (defined below) that may arise between the school and "interested persons" (defined below). The adoption of a Conflict of Interest Policy is an important measure to ensure that senior management act in accordance with their fiduciary duty under state law, that rules applicable to tax-exempt organizations are not violated, and that senior management avoid sanctions for "excess benefit transactions" under Section 4958 of the Internal Revenue Code.

Conflict of Interest Committee. The board may appoint a Conflict of Interest Committee (the "committee") to review information relevant to a request for an advisory opinion or a complaint filed under this policy and to make a recommendation to the board for determination. The recommendation submitted by the committee shall include a summary of the information reviewed and reasons for the recommendation. The board, by majority vote of its members taken in accordance with the school's bylaws, may review the matter as a committee of the whole. The committee shall be composed of the chair and vice chair of the board and one member of the board elected at its annual meeting for a one-year term by a majority vote of the board members in accordance with the voting procedures provided for in the school's bylaws. An alternate to the committee shall be elected for a one-year term at the same time. The alternate shall serve in place of any member of the committee who is unable to serve for any reason including but not limited to being the subject of a conflict of interest issue.

General Policy. All interested persons shall exercise good faith in all transactions relating to their duties to the school and shall not use their positions in any manner that is contrary to the best interests of the school or to promote their own business interests or those of friends or business partners. Moreover, each interested person shall (a) promptly and fully disclose all known and potential conflicts of interest to the head of school and the board or a committee of the board that will consider a contract, transaction, or arrangement to which a known or potential conflict of interest relates (a "contract"), including any relevant facts known to such person regarding a potential conflict of interest; (b) refrain from participating in, or acting on, the decision on any matter in which a conflict of interest, or even the appearance of a conflict of interest, is present with respect to such interested person; and (c) remove himself or herself from any meeting or deliberations on the matter. Any doubts on the part of any interested person as to the existence of, or proper conduct in light of, any perceived conflict of interest should be directed to the head of school and the chair of the board for resolution.

Conflict of Interest Disclosure Statements. Each interested person shall submit an initial statement disclosing any potential or existing conflict of interest upon adoption of this policy or prior to starting his or her position with the school, as applicable. All interested persons shall submit an annual statement, at such time as determined by the school, disclosing any potential or existing conflicts of interest. Such statements shall be submitted to the head of school and the board.

Procedure upon Disclosure of a Potential Conflict of Interest. The board or the committee shall review the information set forth in the request and/or complaint and other reasonably obtainable relevant information and consult with legal counsel. The individual or individuals whose conduct is the subject of the request and/or complaint as well as the individual or individuals making the request and/or complaint are entitled to present information to the board or the committee to assist them in making a determination. Other persons with information that is relevant and of value may be allowed to present such information to the board or the committee. Neither the board nor the committee in its review or consideration of the complaint or request shall be bound by the technical rules of evidence. Determinations regarding conflicts of interest shall be made by the majority vote of the members of the board or the committee in accordance with the voting procedure stated in the bylaws of the school. The board may impose sanctions authorized by this policy upon the determination of a violation of this policy.

Meetings of the board or committee under this policy shall be held in executive session in accordance with all applicable laws.

The board or the committee, as applicable, shall determine, after receiving a disclosure, whether a conflict of interest exists or can reasonably be construed to exist. If a conflict of interest is known or deemed to exist after disclosure, the board or the committee, as applicable, shall not approve the contract with the interested person unless it is determined that (a) entering into such contract is in the best interests of the school, (b) the contract is fair and reasonable to the school, and (c) a more advantageous contract cannot be obtained under the circumstances. Additionally, the board or the committee, as applicable, shall take any action required or prudent to avoid imposition of an excise tax under Internal Revenue Code Section 4958 in connection with considering such contract.

Record Keeping
The board or the committee considering a known or potential conflict of interest matter shall maintain detailed minutes and records regarding the matter. Such minutes shall reflect the name of the interested person and any disclosure made, the vote on whether a conflict of interest is present, the names of the persons participating in any discussions and deliberations with regard to approving or rejecting the contract involving the interested person and the substance of such discussions and deliberations, adherence with the procedures described above, the abstention from voting and participation by the interested person, and that a quorum was present.

Corrective Action. In the event an interested person fails to act in accordance with this Conflict of Interest Policy, the board may take corrective action against him or her. In the event that a formal reprimand or, in an extreme case, the removal of such person from his or her position(s) is proposed, such recommendation must be presented with supporting documentation. The interested person involved shall be given an opportunity to be heard prior to the board's final decision on the matter.

Conflict of Interest Defined. A conflict of interest shall exist in the case of any proposed contract between the school and an interested person or a party with which an interested person has a direct or indirect family, social, or business relationship or financial interest in such contract. For purposes of this Conflict of Interest Policy, a person shall be deemed to have an "interest" in a contract if he or she is a director, trustee, officer, employee, or agent of, or has a significant financial interest in or an influential position with the entity contracting or dealing with the school (other than another entity owned, controlled, or managed by the school).

Interested Person Defined. An interested person is any person who is a trustee, officer, or senior management employee of the school.

Reporting Violations

Your conduct can reinforce an ethical atmosphere and positively influence the conduct of fellow officers and employees. If you are powerless to stop suspected misconduct or discover it after it has occurred, you must report it to the head of school, chair of the Audit Committee, or chair of the board, as appropriate. Reference is made to the school's policy for reporting violations of the Code of Ethics, Code of Conduct, and Conflict of Interest Policy (Whistleblower Protection Policy).

If you are still concerned after speaking with the head of school, chair of the Audit Committee, or chair of the board, or you feel uncomfortable speaking with any of them (for whatever reason, including the involvement of any of them in the conduct which you are reporting), you must (anonymously, if you wish) send a detailed note, with relevant documents, addressed to the board.

Your calls, detailed notes, and emails will be dealt with confidentially. You have the commitment of the school and of the board that you will be protected from retaliation. Reference is made to the school's Whistleblower Protection Policy.

IV. WAIVERS
The school may waive application of the policies set forth in its Code of Ethics, Code of Conduct, and Conflict of Interest Policy only when circumstances warrant granting a waiver and then only in conjunction with any appropriate monitoring of the particular situation. Changes in and waivers of the Code of Ethics, Code of Conduct, and Conflict of Interest Policy may be made only by the board and will be disclosed as required under applicable law and regulations.

V. ADDITIONAL PROVISIONS
You are expected to comply with both the letter and the spirit of all applicable government laws, rules, and regulations.

If you fail to comply with the school's Code of Ethics, Code of Conduct, Conflict of Interest Policy, Whistleblower Protection Policy, and with any applicable laws, you will be subject to disciplinary measures up to and including immediate discharge for employees, removal from office for officers, and removal from the board of trustees.

VI. ADDITIONAL PROVISIONS FOR MEMBERS OF THE BOARD
In addition to the personal and professional ethical responsibilities for senior management stated above, members of the board are expected to understand and comply with legal strictures governing their behavior as described below:

The Standard of Care
Compliance with a standard of care is required by state law. The standard of care encompasses a duty of care, a duty of loyalty, and a duty of obedience. The Code of Ethics and the elements below help fiduciaries meet all three obligations.

The Duty of Care. The satisfaction of the duty of care has three requirements:
- Reasonable and prudent care, informing oneself, and acting in good faith
- Regular attendance at meetings of the board, sharing equally in the work of the board, and exercising independent and informed judgment on all corporate decisions
- Acting in reliance on information and reports received from sources that the board member reasonably regards as trustworthy

The Duty of Loyalty. The duty of loyalty requires trustees to exercise their powers in good faith and in the best interests of the school rather than in their own interest or the interest of another entity or person. The duty of loyalty primarily relates to conflicts of interest and confidentiality.

The Duty of Obedience. To satisfy this duty, the board and individual trustees must be faithful to the purpose and mission of the school as spelled out in the governing documents and mission statement. The board must make sure the school uses its resources appropriately and must monitor the administration to be certain that the school operates within the law, including nonprofit, employment, and other laws.

The Best Interests of the School. Members of the board shall bear in mind the purposes in the school's governing documents. When determining the best interests of the school, each board member must consider the following:
- The purpose of the school to [fill in]
- The school mission to [fill in]
- The school's financial ability to remain viable and to continue to achieve its purpose and mission

In accordance with the foregoing code of conduct, and in addition to the requirements of this code, members of the board are prohibited from the following:

- Making personal criticisms of other board members inside or outside of board meetings
- Discussing the confidential proceedings of the board outside the boardroom or releasing confidential information not previously available to the public by order of the board
- Acting in a way that is actually intended to intimidate another member in the conduct of his or her office or which a reasonable person would conclude had such intent and which, in fact, did intimidate
- Undermining the authority of the board, its chair, or the head of school to perform his or her duties, or interfere with the duties of the school's management and staff
- Committing an act that a person would reasonably expect to cause harm to the reputation of the school or the board
- Speak for or act on behalf of the school unless specifically authorized to do so by the board

ABC SCHOOL
ACKNOWLEDGMENT OF RECEIPT

CODE OF ETHICS, CODE OF CONDUCT, AND CONFLICT OF INTEREST POLICY FOR TRUSTEES, OFFICERS, AND SENIOR MANAGEMENT

I, _____, acknowledge and confirm that I have received a copy of the Code of Ethics, Code of Conduct, and Conflict of Interest Policy for Trustees, Officers, and Senior Management Employees, dated _____, 20___, and have read those standards and do agree that, while I hold a position with the school, I will conduct myself in accordance with those standards.

_____   _____
Witness   Signature

_____
Title/Position

_____
Date

Sample Conflict of Interest Disclosure Statement

A conflict of interest disclosure statement should be completed by each board member, officer, and senior employee once a year. Many boards include blank forms in the materials for the first board meeting after elections and collect the completed forms at the board meeting. If you use this sample policy, be sure to use the name of your school's policy in the first paragraph and replace "ABC School" with the name of your school throughout this document.

ABC SCHOOL
CONFLICT OF INTEREST DISCLOSURE STATEMENT

The undersigned, being a trustee, officer, or senior management employee of ABC School, understands that in order to protect and preserve the tax-exempt status of ABC School, to avoid potential sanctions or adverse rulings, and to otherwise assess the proper operations of ABC School, ABC School has adopted the Code of Ethics, Code of Conduct, and Conflict of Interest Policy for Trustees, Officers, and Senior Management (the "code"). The undersigned acknowledges that he or she has received a copy of the code and has agreed to act in accordance with its standards.

In compliance with the code, the undersigned hereby submits Exhibit A attached hereto as the undersigned's annual disclosure statement indicating all of the undersigned's known and potential conflicts of interest.

Name:_____

Position(s):_____

Dated: _____, 20___

EXHIBIT A
ANNUAL DISCLOSURE STATEMENT

Name:_____
   (Please Print)

REVIEWED BY:
INITIAL: _____   DATE: _____

1. Please state your principal occupation, title (if any), and employer.

2. Please list all *for-profit* organizations, other than that stated in question 1, of which you or a member of your immediate family (spouse, domestic partner, minor child, or other dependent) are a director, officer, or have a significant financial interest. A "significant financial interest" means a financial interest, either directly or indirectly, in the form of a loan, investment, or otherwise that is either more than $10,000 in market value, book value, or face amount or more than 3% of the ownership, capital, or profits interests of a business. A "significant financial interest" *does not include* investment in a security listed on a security exchange unless you also perform services for such entity issuing the security.

3. To the best of your knowledge, do any of the organizations listed in question 1 and 2 or their parents, subsidiaries, sister organizations, or affiliates conduct business transactions with ABC School?

Part 3: Resources, Samples, and Checklists

If yes, which ones and in what manner?

4. Please list all nonprofit organizations (except for ABC School) of which you are a trustee or director, officer, or employee.

5. To the best of your knowledge, do any organizations listed in response to question 4 or their partners, subsidiaries, sister organizations, or affiliates conduct business transactions with ABC School? _____
If so, which ones and in what manner?

6. Based on the definition of "conflict of interest" set forth in the code, please describe any interest you have that may either directly or beneficially give rise to a conflict of interest other than the interests described above.

_____
Name   Signature

_____
Title/Position

Dated: _____, 20__

Sample Whistleblower Protection Policy

This policy provides protection for any employee who reports a violation of a school's Code of Ethics, Code of Conduct, or Conflict of Interest Policy. If you use this sample policy, be sure to replace "ABC School" with the name of your school.

ABC SCHOOL
WHISTLEBLOWER PROTECTION POLICY

Reporting Violations

If any employee reasonably believes that some policy, practice, or activity of ABC School is in violation of a law, rule, regulation, code of ethics, or a clear mandate of public policy, the employee must report such violation to his or her supervisor, the [head of school], or the [board president]. Employees must exercise sound judgment to avoid baseless allegations. An employee who intentionally files a false report of wrongdoing will be subject to discipline up to and including termination.

No Retaliation

The school will not retaliate against any employee who, in good faith, raises a complaint or discloses or threatens to disclose truthful information regarding some practice, policy, or activity of the school or employee of the school the employee reasonably believes violates a law, rule, regulation, or a clear mandate of public policy to (1) a supervisor; (2) an individual with authority to investigate, discover, or terminate misconduct; or (3) a law enforcement officer or public body. The school will also not retaliate against any employee who participates in an investigation relating to some practice, policy, or activity of the school or employee of the school that is or is suspected to be in violation of a law, rule, regulation, or a clear mandate of public policy.

Retaliation includes discharge, demotion, suspension, threats, harassment, or any adverse employment action. Any whistleblower who believes he or she is being subjected to retaliation as a result of whistleblowing activities must contact the [human resources department] or [head of school] immediately.

Confidentiality
Violations or suspected violations may be submitted on a confidential basis or may be submitted anonymously. Reports of violations or suspected violations will be kept confidential to the extent possible. However, identity may have to be disclosed to conduct a thorough investigation to comply with the law and to provide the school and/or accused individuals their legal rights of defense.

Investigation
The Audit Committee of the board of trustees is responsible for investigating and resolving all internal complaints and allegations of financial or accounting impropriety made under this policy. All other complaints will be investigated by the [head of school].

My signature below indicates my receipt and understanding of this policy. I also verify that I have been provided with an opportunity to ask questions about the policy.

Employee Signature   Date

Sample Endowment Policy

This policy assumes that a school has decided to establish an endowment and accept restricted funds into the endowment. The policy references a Gift Acceptance Policy, which can be a separate policy or can be incorporated into the Endowment Policy. The Gift Acceptance Policy is simply a listing of the types of assets that the school will or will not accept for the purpose of establishing an endowment. This policy should be established with the advice of the school's business and financial advisor(s). The board's Investment Committee may be charged with investing the endowment. In cases of large endowments, a separate Endowment Committee may be formed and charged with oversight of investments and expenditures of the school's endowment. If you use this sample policy, be sure to replace "ABC School" with the name of your school.

ABC SCHOOL
ENDOWMENT POLICY

Endowments are a critical element in ABC School's ability to maintain a quality academic program. The school recognizes that each endowment is unique and that exceptions may, from time to time, be appropriate. This Endowment Policy is designed to permit maximum flexibility in securing additional endowment gifts. All endowments will be established in accordance with the school's Gift Acceptance Policy.

The school seeks and receives contributions for the purpose of establishing endowments to fulfill the mission and goals of the institution. Endowments are designated for the following purposes:
- Faculty positions
- Scholarships (and other assistance with tuition, fees, and expenses)
- Programs

The principal of the endowment provides a permanent legacy in support of the school's mission and goals and cannot be drawn down, unless otherwise specified by the donor.

Naming rights (of the endowment, a faculty position, scholarship, or program) should be discussed with the donor prior to accepting the endowment gift. A written endowment gift agreement should be entered into with the donor in all cases but especially when naming rights are concerned. If the donor has named the endowment, a faculty position, scholarship, or program, all staff should be informed of the appropriate method of acknowledging the donor's wishes with respect to naming.

The finance director is responsible for the management of endowment distributions of each of the endowments. The finance director is responsible for ensuring that endowment distributions are used for the purposes intended by the donor in accordance with (a) the donor agreement establishing the endowment and (b) applicable policies approved by the school.

Endowment distributions will be budgeted and used to carry out the school's mission in compliance with the donor's wishes and the school's policies. Expenditures will conform to the school's annual operating budget. No expenditures may be made outside of the annual operating budget without prior board approval.

The finance director or the head of school will approve all expenditures and transfers of funds from the endowment account. Transfers of funds from the endowment account to the school operating account may be made only when the restrictions for the operating account are consistent with the terms of the endowment agreement. Endowment distributions cannot be used to establish or create, in whole or in part, another endowment except in accordance with the school's Gift Acceptance Policy.

Endowment distributions should be expended on an annual basis. When it is impossible or impracticable to use all endowment distributions on an annual basis, accumulations in excess of twice the annual distribution will be reinvested in the corpus of the endowment. Exceptions will be granted by the head of school only on request of the finance director.

The finance director is responsible for preparing and signing an annual year-end report that summarizes the expenditures and transfers from the endowment account. The annual report will also include a brief explanation of how the endowment distribution was used to meet program objectives and donor designations.

The Investment Committee shall oversee the investment of the endowment account to achieve the objective of growth with minimal risk, using such investment vehicles as are appropriate for like endowments.

Sample Record Retention and Disposal Policy

This Record Retention and Disposal Policy covers those records that a school should retain and those that should be disposed of. The key to a successful record retention/disposal policy is making sure that everyone knows about it and then sending out reminders throughout the year to those employees who are charged with overseeing its implementation in their departments. Many organizations make the implementation of their records policy a fun event by providing food and music for an annual records cleanup day when files are marked for retention (and possibly sent off-site for storage) or destroyed. Be sure to have plenty of recycling bins and paper shredders on hand for the cleanup. Ideally your employees will be following the policy all year long and retaining or destroying records according to the policy and the document retention schedule. But an annual cleanup day is sometimes the best way to have everyone comply with the policy.

The records retention schedule is a sample only. You should consult legal counsel in your state for any specific state requirements for record retention, particularly for employment or student records. You should also check any state or federal programs in which your school participates for their required record retention schedules, which will need to be integrated into this sample schedule. If you use this sample policy, be sure to replace "ABC School" with the name of your school.

ABC SCHOOL
RECORD RETENTION AND DISPOSAL POLICY

Purpose
The purpose of this Record Retention and Disposal Policy (the "policy") is to ensure that necessary "records" (as defined below) of the school are adequately protected and maintained and to ensure that records no longer needed or of no value are disposed of at the appropriate time.

The law requires the school to maintain certain types of records, usually for a specified period of time. Failure to retain those records for those minimum periods could subject the school to penalties and fines or charges of destruction of evidence or contempt, cause the loss of legal rights, or significantly impair the school's ability to defend itself in litigation.

Administration

The [title of responsible person] shall be responsible for developing, implementing, and revising this policy governing the retention and disposal of the school's records. He or she will designate others, on an ad hoc basis, to assist in implementing this policy, including the following:

- Identifying and evaluating which records should be retained
- Publishing an appropriate retention and disposal schedule
- Monitoring local, state, and federal laws affecting record retention
- Annually reviewing the record retention and disposal program
- Developing a training program for personnel responsible for record storage and maintenance
- Monitoring for compliance with the record retention and disposal program

Implementation

For purposes of implementing this policy, the school's organizational structure will be segmented into [insert number] departments as follows:

- [list departments by name]

Each department will prepare a listing of major documentation used and maintained by the department and will compare it to the documents listed in this policy. Each department will periodically review currently used records and forms to determine whether these records and forms are adequate and appropriate for the department's requirements.

In addition, each department will periodically review this policy to determine any special circumstances that necessitate changes in the retention periods. Requests for changes in retention periods or deviations from specified retention periods should be made to the [title] and may be implemented only after written approval by the [title] and the school's legal counsel.

In the event of a government audit, investigation, or pending litigation, record disposal may be suspended at the written direction of the [title] or legal counsel. In addition, the [title] or legal counsel should be informed of any situation that might give rise to legal action as soon as the situation becomes apparent. Record disposal after any suspension shall be resumed only at the written direction of the [title] after consultation with the school's legal counsel.

Each department will ensure that its employees are fully informed of this policy and confirm that they agree to comply with this policy. Employees must be informed that any question regarding this policy is to be directed to the [title].

Applicability
This policy applies to all records generated in the course of the school's operations, including both originals and reproductions. It also applies to records stored on computer and microform, electronic mail, and electronic voicemail.

To the extent that there are multiple copies of records, either in paper or electronic form, only one copy of each record need be retained. Likewise, if there are multiple drafts of a particular record, only the final record need be retained, unless such drafts reflect a course of communication by and between the school and non-school personnel.

Retention Periods
From time to time, the school will establish retention or disposal schedules for specific categories of records in order to ensure legal compliance and also to accomplish other objectives, such as preserving intellectual property and managing costs. Several categories of documents are identified in the Appendix.

Definition of "Record"

A "record" is any body of information that has been documented from the business activities of the school, whether in written or electronic form. Examples of "records" include financial data, statements, and associated workpapers; analyses; agreements; books; contracts; charts and tables; data; correspondence and communications that are created, sent, or received; diagrams; electronic messages (email, text messages, and voicemail); images; invoices; letters; logs; maps; memoranda; opinions; plans; projections; statements; studies; and research and any other thing containing information. Examples of what may not be "records" for record retention policies are (a) superseded drafts of documents, including memoranda, financial statements, or regulatory filings; (b) notes on superseded drafts of memoranda, financial statements, or regulatory filings that reflect incomplete or preliminary thinking; (c) previous copies of workpapers that have been corrected for typographical errors or errors due to training of new employees; and (d) duplicates of documents.

A "record" may exist in various forms, including printed, electronic, or recorded format (e.g., letters, email messages, text messages, and voicemail messages). "Records" stored electronically also include records that are stored using equipment located within the school's property or on other devices (whether or not they are owned by the school), such as cellphones, laptops, and tablets. By way of example and not in limitation of the foregoing, the term "record" includes all copies of records made to enable school personnel to work outside school offices.

Record Retention Appendix

Item	Retention Period
Accident reports/claims (settled cases)	7 years
Accounts payable ledgers and schedules	7 years
Accounts receivable ledgers and schedules	7 years
Archive of all website content	7 years
Audit reports	Permanently
Bank statements	7 years
Bank reconciliations	2 years
Bond issuances and ledgers, transfer registers, stubs showing bond issuances, debt issuances, etc.	Permanently
Charts of accounts	Permanently
Checks (cancelled checks for important payments, special contracts, purchase of assets, payment of taxes, etc.); checks should be filed with the papers pertaining to the underlying transaction	Permanently
Checks (cancelled except those noted above)	7 years
Contracts and leases (expired)	7 years
Contracts and leases (still in effect)	Permanently
Corporate minute books	Permanently
Correspondence, general and schedules	3 years
Correspondence, legal and important letters	Permanently
Correspondence, routine with customers/vendors	3 years
Deeds, mortgages, and bills of sale	Permanently
Depreciation schedules	Permanently
Duplicate deposit slips	3 years
Employee personal records (after termination)	3 years
Employment applications (non-hires)	3 years
Financial statements (year-end, other months optional)	Permanently
Financial statements (other)	7 years
General ledgers, year-end trial balances	Permanently
Immigration matters	The longer of (i) entire term of employment plus 1 year or (ii) 3 years

Insurance records, policies, etc.	Permanently
Internal audit reports (miscellaneous)	3 years
Invention/innovation journals (or any other documents or information evidencing creation, modification, or ownership of intellectual properties or other company property)	Permanently
Inventory records	7 years
Invoices to customers or from vendors	7 years
IRA and Keogh plan contributions, rollovers, transfers, and distribution	Permanently
Payroll records, summaries, and tax returns	7 years
Petty cash vouchers	3 years
Property records, including costs, depreciation reserves, year-end trial balances, depreciation schedules, blueprints, and plans	Permanently
Purchase orders	3 years
Receiving sheets	3 years
Retirement and pension records	Permanently
Safety records	7 years
Sales records	7 years
Stock and bond certificates (cancelled)	7 years
Subsidiary ledgers	7 years
Tax returns, revenue agents' reports, and other documents relating to determination of income tax liability	Permanently
Time books, cards, and daily reports	7 years
Trademark registrations, patent letters, and copyright registrations	Permanently
Transcripts	Permanently
Voucher register and schedules	7 years
Vouchers for payments to vendors, employees, etc. (includes allowances and reimbursements of employees, officers, etc., for travel and entertainment expenses)	7 years

Board and Administrative Policy Checklists

Different schools adopt different written policies. Even so, the following lists serve as a useful point of departure for considering the types of policies your board and staff need.

Three efficiency hints:
1. When compiling board meeting minutes, always print statements of board policy in **bold** or CAPITAL LETTERS to make them easily traceable.
2. Simplify the way you track board decisions by creating a cover sheet for each set of minutes with all actions noted and described. This cover sheet can also be kept in a separate file in the school office so that you only need to search one location to find out what was decided when.
3. Make sure that new trustee orientations include either copies of the relevant minutes or a separate policy statement document list, with dates when policies were passed, reaffirmed, etc.

Broad institutional policies for which responsibility rests with the board of trustees:

- [ ] A clear school mission statement, philosophy of education and/or statement of values, and vision statement
- [ ] Up-to-date bylaws
- [ ] Conflict of interest statements (forms that trustees and administrators sign annually to acknowledge the policies and identify real and potential conflicts)
- [ ] Strategic plan with measurable action items (as opposed to operational plans, which are usually the responsibility of the administration and faculty)
- [ ] Rolling three-year financial plan
- [ ] Crisis management plan
- [ ] Authorization or delegation of authority by the board to the head

Part 3: Resources, Samples, and Checklists

Policies for which responsibility rests with the board of trustees and the head:

☐ Safety and security of the school community

☐ Data security

☐ Adequate insurance coverage (including general liability and coverage for directors and officers)

☐ Personnel (including compensation, salary ranges, faculty course load, protection from sexual harassment, whistleblower protection)

☐ Admissions (preferences, if any; desired school population to serve; size of student body)

☐ Financial aid (categories of eligibility; merit or need-based or both)

☐ Financial management, especially checks and balances

☐ Investment management, spending rate, etc.

☐ Bonds for paid staff and volunteers who handle money

☐ Document retention

☐ Bids required for contract goods and services

Risk Management Checklist

Every board should evaluate risk regularly. The following checklist provides a starting point to help you prepare.

- [ ] Clear mission statement
- [ ] Crisis management plan
- [ ] A system to review policies periodically, both internally and with outside professional assistance
- [ ] Up-to-date bylaws
- [ ] A strategic plan that has measurable action plans
- [ ] A rolling three-year financial plan

Adequate insurance:
- [ ] General liability
- [ ] Directors and officers liability

Written policies in these areas:
- [ ] Blood-borne pathogens
- [ ] Conflicts of interest, with forms signed by trustees and administrators acknowledging the policy and identifying potential conflicts
- [ ] Personnel: hiring, evaluation, termination
- [ ] Staff evaluation and compensation (especially in regard to IRS intermediate sanctions provisions)
- [ ] Student code of conduct and discipline procedures
- [ ] Religious activity on campus
- [ ] Athletic safety
- [ ] Use of school bulletin boards
- [ ] Off-campus trips — including policies about adult supervision — locally, nationally, and internationally
- [ ] Use of buildings and grounds by the school community and outsiders
- [ ] Bids required for contracts for goods and services

- ☐ Financial management, especially checks and balances
- ☐ Investment management
- ☐ Admission
- ☐ Financial aid
- ☐ Gift acceptance
- ☐ Bonds for paid staff and volunteers who handle money
- ☐ Publications, videos, and electronic media that portray the school, especially its admission policy, programs, and facilities